1

HEAVEN IS FOR EVERYONE

THIS IS YOUR BOOK OF HEAVEN

~ ENCOURAGEMENT FOR YOU ~

HEAVEN IS FOR EVERYONE

Trenee' Zweigle, RN

Table of Contents

Let the Universe proclaim His Name

HEAVEN IS FOR EVERYONE!

~ PREPARE YOUR HEART ~

Look

Jesus is Coming

With the clouds

And every eye

Will see Him ...

Revelation 1:7

Jesus lovingly holds out His nail scarred hands to you and throws open the gates of Heaven, beckoning you to come home to live in peace and safety forever. **He doesn't want even one single person to miss out** on all the beautiful, incredible, fantastic, and amazing things in Heaven He has created just for you. Everyone will get along in harmony and love, sharing and enjoying life together.

💕 "For God so loved the world, that he gave his only Son, that **whoever believes in him should not perish but have eternal life**." John 3:16

💕 "The Lord is not slow about His promise, but is patient toward you, **not willing for any to perish**, but for all to come to repentance." 2 Peter 3:9

However, He doesn't use force to anyone, not ever. It needs to be totally their own choice and His heart breaks every day when thousands of people deny Him, or say He doesn't exist, or turn their back on Him. Some people may think "Well, I'm a construction worker, what would I do in Heaven?!"

It doesn't matter if you're a logger, doctor, construction engineer, nurse, teacher, veterinarian, cashier, secretary, trucker, or any of thousands of other jobs—He will have such incredible things for you to happily do and keep busy with creativity that you won't believe it. They say if you have a job you love, then you will never work a day in your life —because it's not work for you.

You'll be having fun in heaven with a fantastic day every single day. Not only that, but you can learn anything you would like to since there will be no mental roadblocks and no restrictions to hold you back. Everyone will have equal capabilities and opportunities to learn and do whatever they like, and everyone has different ideas and personalities; that will never change. We can't even begin to imagine all the various things He has in store for us to explore—it's too far above our comprehension!

What does God say to you about Heaven?

He would say:

"I just can't wait to hear your healthy, happy, cheerful voices resounding through Heaven and the universe in praise, wonder and joy! Your squeals and cheers of delight as you see and experience awesome new things. When you greet your angel with love and meet all the incredible hosts of Heaven. As you taste new fruits and foods.

As you hug and love amazing new animals you have never seen before. When you realize there is no darkness and no fear. Your eyes will widen with wonder as you gaze at all the beautiful and unique things surrounding you.

I have made so many exquisite and truly amazing things for you, it will be my long-awaited pleasure and joy to introduce you to all I have created and saved for you. I am looking forward to showing you each one of them—also to give you the best hug of your entire life!"

"My help comes from the Lord who made Heaven and earth." Psalm 121:2

WELL, HOW DO WE GET THERE?

How do we even get to Heaven? What do we have to do? Jesus says:

💕 "I am the way, the truth, and the life: The only way to come to My Father is to come to Him through Me." John 14:6

Jesus willingly gave up His own life for each and every single one of us, and He died on the cross in order for us to be given eternal life. A life with no fear, no worries, no losses, no confusion or panic. There will be no misunderstandings, no arguments or fights. No competing to be the most important and best, because our goal will be to lovingly help and teach others along the way. You are continuously in His heart and in His mind. He wants so very much for you to be in Heaven with Him forever.

At His death Jesus looked toward heaven and prayed:

"Father, the hour has come. Glorify your Son, that your Son may glorify you.

² For you granted him authority over all people that he might give eternal life to all those you have given him.

³ Now this is eternal life: that they know you, the only true God, and Jesus Christ, whom you have sent.

⁴ I have brought you glory on earth by finishing the work you gave me to do. ⁵ And now, Father, glorify me in your presence with the glory I had with you before the world began.

⁶ I have revealed you to those whom you gave me out of the world. They were yours; you gave them to me, and they have obeyed your word.

⁷ Now they know that everything you have given me comes from you.

⁸ For I gave them the words you gave me, and they accepted them. They knew with certainty that I came from you, and they believed that you sent me." John 17:1-8

DID YOU KNOW JESUS PRAYS FOR YOU?

Did you know that Jesus even prays over you for protection from harm and from the evil one? Even though sometimes we may forget to keep in touch with Him or those we love or care about, Jesus will never forget you or forget to pray for you. He loves you so much He knows everything about you, the bible says He has even counted every hair on your head! All you need to do is ask Him to pray for you, and for your understanding in all that He wants to share with you—but don't say it with a question mark, you need to really sincerely mean it. Jesus said:

"Your Father knows the things you have need of before you ask Him."
Matthew 6:8 NKJV

"Father, I want those you have given me to be with me where I am (in Heaven), and to see my glory, the glory you have given me because you loved me before the creation of the world. Righteous Father, though the world does not know you, I know you, and they know that you have sent me. I have made you known to them, and will continue to make you known in order that the love you have for me may be in them and that I myself may be in them." John 17: 25, 26

"Therefore, he is able to save **forever** those who come to God through him, because he always lives to intercede for them." Hebrews 7:25

So, when the devil knocks at the door just ask Jesus to answer it! Jesus always refers to God's Word, with the character and essence of God. He loves to manifest the heart of God through His Word.

Jesus's view of scripture meant He centered everything in His life on the Words of God. (The Bible)

💕 **"I have given to them the Words which You have given Me; and they have received them." John 17:8**

Everyone knew the heart of Jesus because of the words He spoke. There is no shortcut to Heaven or God's Word. We need to put our heart and soul into His truth, into His hands, and receive His blessings in reading the bible. He has the words of LIFE through His Son Jesus who quoted the scriptures frequently. Jesus totally believed and lived every single word of the bible; he told others of scripture every day. He **knew** for certain that people can know and see their Father in heaven by thoughtfully reading the bible scriptures. To get the biggest blessing of our lives, we need to read the bible through the eyes and understanding Jesus had when He read them Himself.

As we all know, Love is spelled out many different ways: in actions, words, examples, giving, listening, and much more. God poured out His heart to us in all these ways as well. He has created the most incredible creatures, animals, flowers, plants, sky, stars, whispering breezes, fluttering leaves on beautiful trees, others to love us. There are many more people than you even know who love you right now. He is saying: *LOVE ME, LOVE MY WORDS TO YOU! I LOVE YOU MORE THAN ANYONE ELSE EVER POSSIBLY COULD OR EVER WILL. I HAVE CREATED MANY EXQUISITE THINGS JUST FOR YOU TO ENJOY.*

WE ARE BROKEN

So why should we seek Jesus and God, His face, His love, and His words in the Bible? **Because we are broken!** We are broken in so many ways there are no words to describe it. And for each one of us it is different because we all see things differently, feel things in a different way...but it all hurts to the core of our being just the same. It affects our mental status, emotional status, physical being, family, friends, financial, work ethics and so much more. The **great** news for us is that **Jesus' broken body put an end to our brokenness. That doesn't mean it was easy for Him, not at all. The only thing we need to do is accept Him and follow Him. He asks us to read His words in the bible and reach out for Him to speak to our hearts. He could have given 1000 Commandments for us to get there, but He only gave us 10, to make our lives much better, happier and contented.**

He just loved each one of us so much that He endured what needed to be done by dying on the cross so that you could live in Heaven forever in love, joy, peace, comfort, happiness with no fear. Can you even imagine no fear? It stalks us like a shadow everywhere we go. The smallest snap, crunch or unexpected sound will startle us into full alert mode, even when we're asleep. But in Heaven we will have no fear— ever!

Commit thy way unto the Lord; trust also in Him; and He shall bring it to pass. Psalm 37:5

HEAVEN IS WAITING FOR YOU

Who is God, Jesus, and the Holy Spirit?

How are they described?

Everyone wants to know! Many thousands of people have had "close to death" experiences from near drownings to traumatic accidents and injuries. Each one of them happened differently, but every single survivor has said the same thing: God is _not_ an uninterested and distant "entity." He does not stand off in the distance being judgmental while shaking His finger at you. He doesn't leave you standing there feeling exposed, naked and at fault for every single thing you ever did wrong. Quite the opposite. God, Jesus, and the Holy Spirit are One Trinity, completely surrounding you with unconditional light and love—always supportive and encouraging.

Everyone who has felt they were in His presence did not feel a sense of trauma or pain, just a feeling of warmth, love, tenderness and complete acceptance into His arms of love which completely envelopes and surrounds them. It's a phenomenon not fully understood, but there are many thousands of testaments to this. Visualizing Heaven, there was **not** a feeling of wanting to return to life as it has been for them on earth, only a desire to continue on into the awesome Kingdom of God to remain in His beautiful warm glowing light/presence and love forever. When returned to their earth y life, they were very disappointed. Many stated they were given specific reasons of why they were being returned and assignments to help family, friends and others, and to spread the word of His soon return (as states in the Bible is now imminent.) He wants all to know that their entrance to Heaven is FREE because it was purchased by the death of HIS son so that anyone who wants to accept it will be given eternal life with Him. **"For God so loved the world (meaning you) that He gave His only begotten Son, that whoever (you) believes in Him will not perish but will have eternal life." John 3:16**

Others non-verbally immediately knew of ways to improve their lives and how to reach out to others in encouragement to live their lives with

God and Jesus, and to look forward to His return to take all who want to go home to Heaven where they ultimately belong. Previously they had gone their own ways but never felt fulfilled or truly happy. After their experience all stated they had a completely new understanding of life's meaning and felt a need and desire to be in Heaven with God, Jesus, and the Holy Spirit—plus all the hosts of Heaven forever.

What is *absolutely amazing* is that **each of these near-death survivors describes the same things**, only in different words or terminology. Basically, the core of their "out of body" experience of seeing or being in heaven is *described as follows*:

1. Each individual is connected with indescribable total love which far exceeds anything we have ever felt on earth in any relationship or form and is felt unanimously by everyone. Not one person is ever left out or made to feel inferior to anyone else.

2. Verbal language is not necessary since everything in heaven is exponentially advanced and much higher on all levels than what we know or have experienced. God of the universe is the essence of love, communicates directly with each person non-verbally which permeates the core of their body and soul in the most incredibly delightful, comforting, and all-knowing manner.

3. There is no jealousy or anger in heaven, therefore no contention or fighting. Each person or being has the utmost love and desire to help others, make them comfortable and to exceed in all their goals or endeavors as if it were their own.

4. The colors, sights, sounds, fragrances are heightened and expanded in ways that are indescribable; it is possible to **feel** them as well as visualize and hear everything.

5. There is fantastic music in heaven with incredible choirs, and every single person or being in heaven has the ability to sing, as well as play any instrument they would like. There are no exhausting "training" lessons, it is a natural gift, the same as a given instant knowledge in building your own house or creating a botanical garden if you like, plus so much more.

Those who have come back from near-death experience have said to others who may not believe them: "Why would you **ever** take a chance on missing out on something so real and awesome as this, when all you need to do is believe in God?" (Most who had these experiences did not previously know about God or had not made any effort to do so.)

Why would God love us that much and fight for us to be in Heaven forever with Him, and give us awesome gifts with a blessed life? Many have just figured out for the very first time that God is our only real true Father/Parent with pure and good intentions, and for many of us He's our *only* Father for many reasons—plus He created us. Parents who really love their children (including those with "fur-babies" who they love as children) would do anything they could for them to have healthy, happy lives with everything they could possibly give them. Explode that amount times infinity and that's how much your Heavenly Father loves you, also why He wants you to have so much more.

Psychologists, ministers, and those who study near death experiences have acknowledged the credibility of such profound encounters and have stated that although each may be presented differently there can be no denial that God exists and has love beyond description. These near deaths have occurred in many walks of life including children, farm workers, pastors, doctors and nurses, some working in the Trade Center during the collapse of the building, scientists, illiterate, highly educated, and even tribe natives who had never even heard of God or Jesus.

Many have also tried to denounce or deny Him. One well respected man named *Lee Strobel* was a Yale-educated, award-winning journalist at the Chicago Tribune. As a self-declared atheist, he decided to compile a legal case against Jesus Christ and prove beyond any argument that He was not God or anything more than an average man, which would be presented by the weight of the accumulated evidence he was determined to find.

As Legal Editor of the Tribune, Strobel's area of expertise was courtroom analysis. To make his case against Christ, Strobel cross-examined a number of Christian authorities, recognized experts in their own fields of study (including PhD's from such prestigious academic centers as Cambridge, Princeton, and Brandeis). He conducted his examination with no religious bias, other than his predisposition to atheism.

Quite remarkably, after diligently compiling and critically examining the evidence for himself, Strobel became a Christian. Stunned by his findings, he organized all the "evidence" into a fascinating book he wrote entitled, "***The Case for Christ***", proving the fact that there **is** a God! The book won the Gold Medallion Book Award for excellence. Strobel asks one thing of each reader—remain unbiased in your examination of the evidence (the Bible.) There are millions of other testimonials as well. God's door is **always** open to His children.

Those who have studied God's Word in the Bible know that there is a "Trinity" which consists of God our Father and Creator, Jesus our Savior who died on the cross for each of us, and the Holy Spirit our Comforter, Guide, Leader and Communicator. If we sincerely pray and ask Him to reveal to us things from the Bible we don't understand, He will do so. He holds the key to all communication and assists in our entrance to heaven by showing us the way.

Just as a united strong family is one family, it consists of several people, and each one has their own unique personality and way of doing things. They may be in different areas doing different things, but they are still one family and stay in tune or constant contact with each other. The same applies to The Trinity who is united as one strong unit, but each has an assignment to fulfill, and each has the same desire for us to be in Heaven forever in peace, harmony and joy. We will all succeed and excel at all we accomplish because of Them.

God the Trinity:

God the Father

God the Son   **God the Holy Spirit**

Does He really care?

Does He really know who I am?

Yes! He certainly does. He created each of us to be *totally different*, complex and unique, each is intricately created. Every fiber and cell in our body is electrifying and amazing. Not even twins or triplets are exactly the same. Yet have you ever felt vastly insignificant, alone and forgotten? Do you wonder if anyone even remembers your name? Do you feel so small and unimportant that you are afraid to even ask to "take some of God's time" or "bother Him?" You figure He's busy running the universe and has pretty big top priority jobs, so why would you even matter? Sometimes it's easy to feel "down and out" and stomped on by the entire world. But there is someone who **does** know your name and even has your name carved permanently in the palm of His hand! Everything is under control, He's got you. Not only that, but He would also love to have a relationship with **you**! While you are sitting there afraid to even speak, He is standing in front of you with his arms of love extended out to you. Don't ever think He is too busy running the world, because He has all the time in the world just for **you**. It's no problem whatsoever for Him to multi-task! Yes, He already knows everything about you, just reach out to Him.

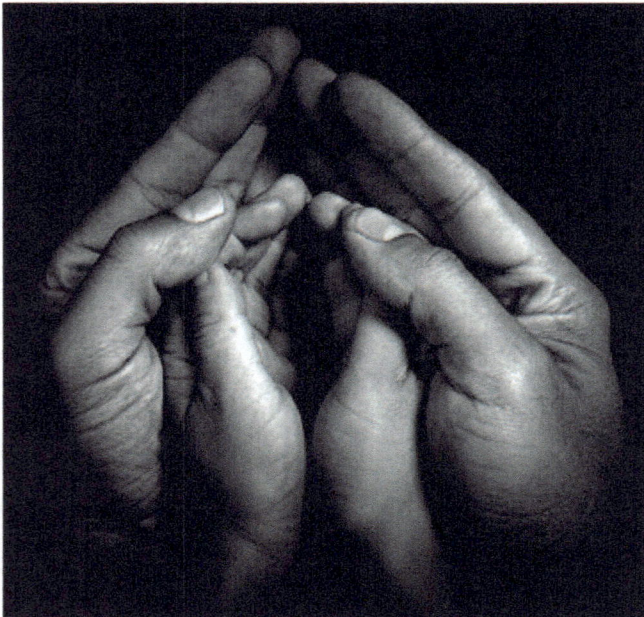

"I **have written your name** on the **palms of my hands.**" Isaiah 49:16

There is a great song by Francesca Battistelli which says, "Make no mistake, He knows my name." It's such a beautiful and encouraging song. (Partial lyrics below)

Francesca Battistelli - He Knows My Name

Spent today in a conversation
In the mirror face to face

With somebody less than perfect,
I wouldn't choose me first

If I was looking for a champion
In fact I'd understand

If You picked everyone before me
But that's just not my story

True to who You are
You saw my heart
And made
Something out of nothing.

I don't need my name in lights—
I'm famous in my Father's eyes
Make no mistake,
He knows my name
I'm not living for applause
I'm already so adored.

I'm not meant to just stay quiet
I'm meant to be a lion
I'll roar beyond a song
With every moment that I've got

I don't need my name in lights
I'm famous in my Father's eyes
Make no mistake,
He knows my name.

Not only does God know **your** name, but He also knows every single thing about you. He knows your likes and dislikes, your heart of love…and He's totally in love with **you**! He thinks you're awesome, and He knows how creative, amazing, intelligent, kind and helpful you are. He knows all the things you are capable of doing and has plans forever for you in heaven. He has supplies for every invention, every farm, every desire, every building, every animal and bird, every project you could ever think of or imagine—He's got you covered! Heaven will **not** be a boring, quiet, dismal place to tiptoe around. Far from it, heaven will be teaming with activity, togetherness, boisterous laughing. Even the most limited of us will then be able to hop, skip, dance, invent things of our wildest dreams, and be surrounded with people who really love us and are truly interested in absolutely everything we are and do. They will be cheering us on, just as we will be cheering them on!

But that's not all, it gets even better and better. Did you know He loves you so much that He has counted every single hair on your head, and all the hairs you previously had on your head?! He knows all the core desires of your heart and great accomplishments you desperately want to make. So, do you know of anyone else who has ever been able to do that, or even cared to? You mean so much to Him and are so special to Him that He would have died on the cross *JUST FOR YOU ALONE*! He would do anything necessary to bring you home to be with Him forever to have the most beautiful home you have ever imagined, surrounded by perfect trees, jungle plants, flowers, rivers and streams. All the things that inspire you and make you happy. He has plans for you that even in your wildest dreams you couldn't imagine how awesome they are and how happy you will be. A relationship with God, Jesus, and the Holy Spirit fills life with joy, peace and love both now and for eternity.

Can you even imagine everything being *PERFECT*? No brown rotting vegetation, no crippled people or animals, no death or dying, no leaves falling off the trees! No polluted water with decaying fish, trash, and plastic bags—no "global warming" or pandemics. No arguing or disagreements, no fear of World War III. Yes, everyone will have different ideas about things, but they'll be able to work together on all of it for a great solution and great benefit of blessings for everyone.

Many more loved ones and angels will be surrounding you, because everything and everyone in heaven is about LOVE. There will be peace, harmony, HUGS, encouragement, happiness, and pure joy.

Each one of us wonders many times in our lives what we did wrong to deserve something negative or devastating while walking through a storm. We may wonder if God took a step backwards, got busy elsewhere, or entirely forgot about us. Always remember that you are a precious and much-loved child of God, and that is the devil talking when those unhappy thoughts enter your mind. If someone took a step backwards, guess who it was?

Also remember that death, tragedy, wars, impure or negative thoughts and actions all come from Satan—so give credit where credit is due.

But God has provided a way through it all for us. Walking through a storm is the only way to build faith and character; we go through trials to strengthen our stand for Him, and He will always bring us out on the winning side some way and bless us to help others through it all. People know you understand when you've been through what they are going through, you can help ease their pain and discouragement. He is right there with us every step of the way. There are many stories of God's wondrous miracles and how much He loves us unconditionally.

You have probably seen a tiny acorn. But that small insignificant acorn can turn into a beautiful mighty oak tree. To arrive at that point, it must go through rain, wind, sleet, snow, storms and adverse situations to build up its powerful strength which enables it to withstand drastic conditions. **We are like that acorn turning into a mighty oak tree**. We can give up and fall over, or we can take each issue to God, fully knowing He will bring us through it. His love and protection are more powerful than any storm we can ever face, and He will bring something good from it. *We may never see all the good that comes from it, but it's like a ripple in the lake that goes on and on to help others.*

We can become His mighty oak trees!

Some people may be thinking: "But I've done such horrible things throughout my life that God certainly wouldn't want me to be in Heaven! I don't have even the slightest chance of going home to Heaven." Well, let's think about this for a moment. Did Jesus leave the comfort of heaven to come to a sinful planet of filth and corruption to save the holy? Did He come to save the saved?

No! There would be no need for Him to go through all He went through and die to save those who were already saved. He came to seek and to save those who would be lost for eternity, those who were at the bottom of the trash pile in sin. There is story after story in the Bible of those He spent time with; they were healed and forgiven, saved for eternity.

And that's exactly how many of us have felt—unworthy of anything good, beyond any hope of ever seeing heaven or actually seeing God smile at us, let alone go to the cross to die for us so that He could welcome us with open loving arms into His Kingdom of heaven to be with Him forever.

But that's exactly what He did, and He will not leave **anyone** out if they want to change their life and come home with Him. He was more than willing to do whatever was needed to provide a fantastic life in Heaven just for you. He's counting on you to be there!

Does He really want **you** to be there with Him? Absolutely! He has gone out of His way to provide the most extraordinary and wonderful life for you with special things to keep you fascinated and busy each and every day.

Heaven is not boring, you will be captivated with such interesting things that appeal specifically to you, not necessarily to everyone else. God knows exactly what you are intrigued with, and He will expand your horizons to the maximum, more than you could ever imagine!

Birds and all creatures call out to Him in praise.

The things He has created will lift your spirits and sometimes bring you to your knees. All the new colors to experience along with textures, lighting, sights, sounds, feelings, comprehension, understanding, communication plus so much more.

Artist version of heavenly clouds with kitten

Everything we can imagine is possible. There are so many millions of things we have never seen or even thought of which are created by the hand of God. They are beautiful, intricate, minutely detailed. Our minds won't be able to keep up with all the incredible creations: plants, trees, animals, foods, games, music, sports, architecture and so much more. There will be so much to see and do, you will feel like your mind is exploding with joy.

BEAUTIFUL SCENERY WILL BE EVERYWHERE

How do we know which way to go or what to do next?

It's very simple, He always has a plan for us:

💕 *"I will instruct thee and teach thee in the way which thou shalt go;*

I will guide thee with my eye." **Psalms 32:8**

💕 *"I know the plans I have for you says the Lord, plans not to harm*

you but to bring you hope and a future." **Jeremiah 29:11**

We are the wonderful mixture in His flower garden

Each one of us is so different, just like each one of His creations and flowers.   Yet each is so very special!

But what if I don't feel His love?

What if I don't matter?

<u>Everyone matters to God</u>! He loves you so very much that Jesus died on the cross just for you, so that you could have an eternal life of love, security, peace and safety. All of us feel insecure at some point in our lives, some feel that acutely more than others. But never listen to Satan's lies, because all negatives come from him. In every situation of life, he wants you to believe that you are "less" than everyone else, that you don't count for anything.

One of his greatest tools is discouragement and depression along with thoughts of negativity we accept about ourselves—it certainly puts a big smile on his ugly face. The very second you have any bad thoughts about yourself ask God to take them from you and for Him to kick the devil out of your life (and away from those you love and care about.) Remember, God will always fill in all the blank pages and empty spaces in our lives with good things...all we need to do is ask Him.

"YOU SAY" Lauren Daigle

There is an awesome song by Lauren Daigle called "You Say" that would bless you to hear on the internet or elsewhere, and below are partial lyrics provided by courtesy of Internet © Appstreet Music, Centricsongs

I keep fighting voices in my mind that say I'm not enough
Every single lie that tells me I will never measure up
Am I more than just the sum of every high and every low
Remind me once again just who I am because I need to know

You say I am loved when I can't feel a thing
You say I am strong when I think I am weak
And you say I am held when I am falling short
And when I don't belong, oh You say I am Yours

And I believe
Oh, I believe
What You say of me
I believe

The only thing that matters now is everything You think of me
In You I find my worth, in You I find my identity
Taking all I have, and now I'm laying it at Your feet
You have every failure, God, You have every victory

You say I am loved when I can't feel a thing
You say I am strong when I think I am weak
You say I am held when I am falling short
When I don't belong, oh You say I am Yours
And I believe - Oh, I believe

STORMS OF LIFE

Have you ever been through a major storm in your life and wondered how you would ever get through it? Did you feel so alone you thought nobody cared or would come to your defense? There is someone who loves and cares about you more than you could ever imagine, and he is seldom spoken of. He is part of the Trinity of Heaven, and he wants to be with you twenty-four/seven to lead, guide, strengthen and comfort you.

He is the Holy Spirit who is very sensitive and acutely feels everything that you are going through. Just as with having Jesus as your partner, the Holy Spirit is not someone you can absent-mindedly call on once in a great while.

He wants to be right by your side to help you make the right decisions, and to bring you through any painful trials or storms of life. You will be so happy to get to know him, and the same as with any family members or someone you love, you need to communicate closely with him all day long every day. He will make all the great and positive differences in your life.

Our Trinity: God the Father, Jesus (God the Son) and the Holy Spirit are each unique individuals, yet they are One in loving us, caring for us, and providing a way for us each step of our lives. Sometimes we get off the path into a tangled briar patch and we can't see any way out of it. Have you ever felt so hurt or so invisible that you just want to run and **hide** far out of the way?

All we need to do is reach up and God is more than happy and willing to lift us up on high out of harm's way. Yet there **is** a place we can hide in safety, where we are warm and cuddled, a place we are so loved and appreciated beyond anything we could imagine—in the arms of our Father and Savior.

There is a beautiful song that will take you from any storm straight to a place of peace, harmony, tranquility, calmness, and the feeling of total acceptance: "**You are my hiding place**." Listen to different versions and allow it to speak to your heart. We can't see the air we breathe, but we know it exists or we wouldn't be alive! Just the same way, we need to trust the fact that we are accepted, much loved, and very precious to the King of the Universe.

Transitioning to peace and calm "Peace, be still." Mark 4:39

Jesus is all about peace and calm, and He is mentioned 953 times in the bible regarding peace. If He tells us almost 1000 times in one book (the Bible) of how important peace is, then it is definitely true. That includes peace in our hearts as well as peace and calm around us. Any time we truly cry out to God, He is always there listening to every word we speak, every need that we have. Does He say anything about doing it all alone by ourselves or struggling much harder? No! He is our hiding place and will wrap us tightly in His strong arms of love. He even says: "I will fight for you, all you need is be still." Exodus 14:14

What does the calming of the storm teach us about Jesus?

Jesus calming the storm is a demonstration of His Majestic power, not only can He walk upon the tumultuous water, but it must bow to his commands and obey. But more than that it shows us that God sees what we are going through. It tells us that **He knows our fears and pain and that we can never be out of His arms or left all alone**.

Millions of people have felt this deeply from the core of their soul and have written the most beautiful and meaningful praise and worship songs ever written. One of these is an old-time favorite Christian song "_You Are My Hiding Place_." It has been sung by many different artists in solos, duets, and choirs—but especially touches your heart with the background music, it's worth looking up and listening online or even purchasing some praise worship CD's or DVD's. You can also listen to K-LOVE Radio station or HOPE Radio station for comfort, peace and joy. There is a hiding place of peace, calm, and tranquility in the Lord.

You Are My Hiding Place

You are my hiding place
You always fill my heart
With songs of deliverance
Whenever I am afraid,

    I will trust in You
    I will trust in You
    Let the weak say
    I am strong
    In the strength of the Lord.

        You are my hiding place
        You always fill my heart
        With songs of deliverance
        Whenever I am afraid

            I will trust in You
            I will trust in You
            Let the weak say I am strong
            In the strength of the Lord
            I will trust in You

                You are my hiding place
                You always fill my heart
                With songs of deliverance
                Whenever I am afraid.

Any time you are feeling insignificant and need to know how very much God loves and wants you to be His own child forever. **He will always hold you in the palm of His hand!** Here are the lyrics to "You Can Rest."

You Can Rest — Hillary Scott

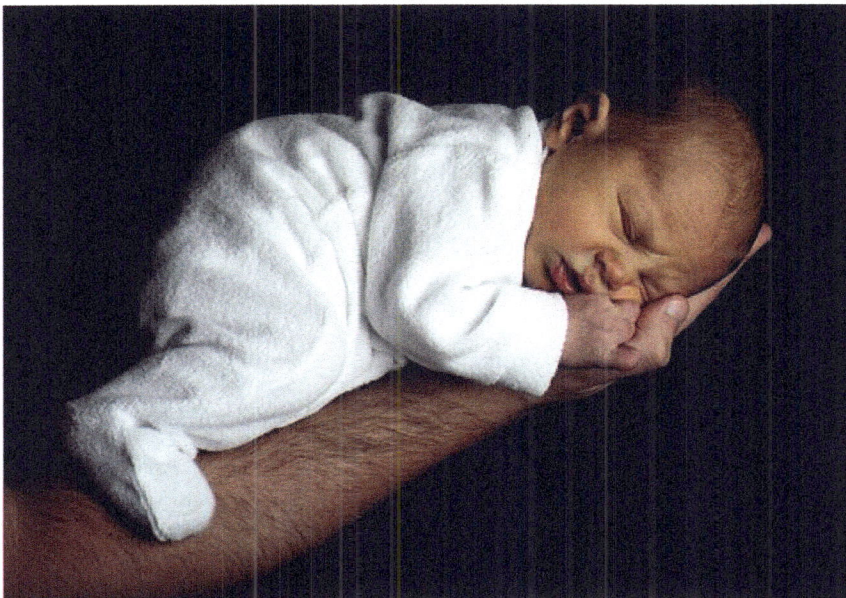

When your weary
heart is hurting or
you're feeling so
alone
When you think that
you're a burden or
nowhere feels like
home
When everything
feels like it's
changing, and you
don't understand
why
Trying so hard to be
strong and brave but
so tired you wanna
cry
Don't forget as you

fall asleep to lay it all at the Father's feet

You can rest, you can rest

In the one who never breaks His promises
Close your eyes, talk to Him
When you're scared and feel the darkness rolling in
In your worry and your pain, just breathe in and out His name
Jesus, oh, Jesus
And you can rest

When you're looking in the mirror and you're struggling to believe
Am I really who He says I am, or will God give up on me?
When anxiety is yelling and it's drowning out today
When it's hard to see tomorrow and you don't know how to pray

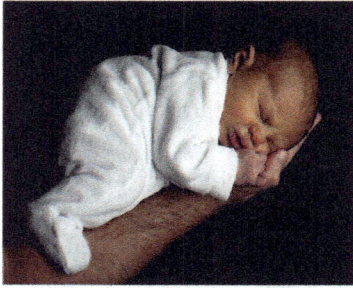

You can rest, you can rest
In the one who never breaks His promises
Close your eyes, talk to Him
When you're scared and feel the darkness rolling in
In your worry and your pain, just breathe in and out His name:

Jesus, oh, Jesus
And you can rest
You can rest

Don't forget as you fall asleep
You are safe at the Father's feet

You can rest, you can rest
 In the one who never breaks His promises
Just close your eyes and talk to Him
When you're scared and feel the darkness rolling in

In your worry and your pain,
just breathe in and out His name
Jesus, Jesus
Oh, Jesus
And you can rest
You can rest.

And if you should ever feel *lost*, no worries because God is looking for **you**. He treasures you, loves you, and will stop at nothing to rescue you if you are looking for Him too—just send out an SOS!

He is a roaring Lion who is seeking to destroy your enemies and to protect you.

Here are lyrics to Rescue by Lauren Daigle:

RESCUE

Lauren Daigle

You are not hidden
There's never been a moment
You were forgotten
You are not hopeless
Though you have been broken,
Your innocence stolen

I hear you whisper underneath your breath
I hear your SOS, your SOS

I will send out an army to find you
In the middle of the darkest night
It's true, I will rescue you

There is no distance
That cannot be covered
Over and over

You're not defenseless
I'll be your shelter
I'll be your armor

I hear you whisper underneath your breath
I hear your SOS, your SOS

I will send out an army to find you
In the middle of the darkest night

It's true, I will rescue you
I will never stop marching to reach you
In the middle of the hardest fight
It's true, I will rescue you

I hear the whisper underneath your breath
I hear you whisper you have nothing left

I will send out an army to find you
In the middle of the darkest night
It's true, I will rescue you
I will never stop marching to reach you
In the middle of the hardest fight
It's true, I will rescue you

Oh, I will rescue you

He puts such intricate detail into each creation

Peacocks and birds tell of God's love and intricate designs

His animals, creatures, and creations are exquisite

God's Handiwork stands Forever

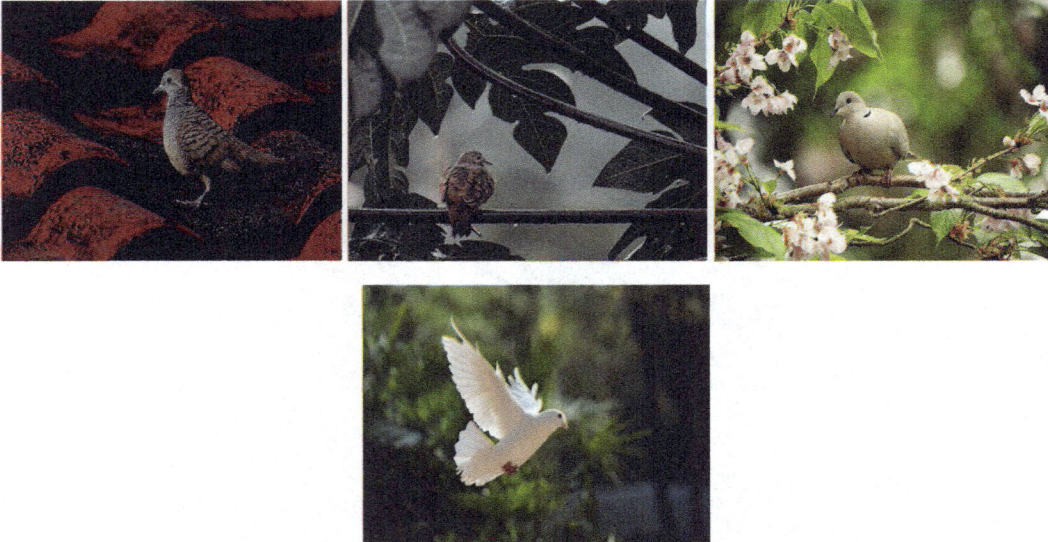

The Dove

When God makes a point to you, He usually backs it up a few times, so always be in tune to His leading. There was a pastor who especially loved birds and even went on excursions to photograph or observe them. One day while out on a drive he noticed a lonely yet beautiful dove on a telephone line. He looked around for a flock of birds, or at least a mate—but there was just the one lonely dove. He pondered that for a while, then drove on to his destination. He always kept his heart and mind open to the Lord to reveal things to him, and for some reason he kept thinking about that dove. Several days later while on the way to a friend's house in another location he saw the dove on a rooftop sitting alone, but no other doves nearby. He kept looking for its family as he continued on, but none were seen.

The following week as the minister drove to town, he saw the lonely dove once again just sitting all by himself. Off in the distance black storm clouds were gathering with a few streaks of sunlight, and a misty rain began to fall. The dove didn't leave, but just sat there in the growing rainstorm with gloom surrounding it, and in the background began thunder and lightning.

The minister thought how beautiful, peaceful, and majestic the dove looked in spite of the impending disaster, then suddenly it hit him. Jesus was represented by the dove of peace, and God sent down a beautiful dove to claim Him as the Son of God, our messiah. Jesus associated with others to bring the message of love, heaven, and eternal life—but much of His life he spent alone, then He went to the cross alone where He died in our place to freely give **us** the gift of heaven forever!

The pastor pulled over to the side of the road, tears were running down his cheeks while feeling the ache in his heart for all that Jesus went through. Weeks later there was sunshine, with signs of new life and the pastor saw a beautiful dove in a tree surrounded with blossoms. He thought to himself now that appropriately represented Jesus's resurrection and giving new life to us.

Yes, **Heaven is for everyone**, and He doesn't want anyone to be left out. All we need to do is believe in Him and He will give His free gift to us, the gift of eternal life in heaven with Him. We need to read the directions in the manual which is called the Book of Life—God's Word in the bible.

We are His Oak Trees

Beautiful flowers will never fade or die

We will stand in the arbor of eternal life,

enjoying His creations forever

Light green, dark green, and dewdrops—

All part of God's handiwork made just for you

We will run carefree through fields of Poppies

Sunshine Poppies Forever!

Heaven will always be about light, happiness, cheer, and awesome times—with no fear ever again. It's all about sharing, loving and caring.

His creations will never cease to amaze us

Beautiful streaming sunlight forever!

Comforting jungle foliage for our enjoyment

It will always be springtime, no storms!

Beautiful Blossoms forever, they will never fade

Heaven's nature and trees will take your breath away

💕 "Yours, Oh Lord, are the greatness, the power, the glory, the victory and the majesty; for all that is in the heavens and on the earth is Yours." 1 Chronicles 29:11

Almighty God, we need to tell you more often how awesome You are. We stand before you in complete humble awe of your creations, sovereignty, and all Your power. Let us remember that when it comes to moving mountains and calming storms that You, Lord, are the one and only God—and we give you praise, honor and glory at all times.

Note: "If God is willing to move your mountain, don't pipe up and tell him where you think it should be placed!"

♥ "Be strong and courageous; do not be frightened or dismayed, for the Lord your God is with you wherever you go." Joshua 1:9

Lord Father, it's such a blessing to know that no matter where I'm going or what I'm doing, and no matter how close to the edge I get, You are right there with me. You never have a scheduling conflict even though You're running the world. Thank you for always being there with me, there are so many days that I can't take a single step without leaning on You.

♥ "Let us not grow weary in doing what is right, for we will reap at harvest time if we do not give up." Galatians 6:9

♥   **Heart-Note**: "Fear is failure to give faith its rightful place in our hearts. Stand up straight right now and Praise Him!"

Many Blessings Are Waiting for you!

Soft breezes whisper the name of Jesus and testify of His continuous love. His voice is the one you hear whispering to your heart when you need strength, guidance someone to love you unconditionally—no matter what you've ever done. There is no condemnation, only a gentle voice saying:

"Come to me, all of you who are weary and burdened, and I will give you rest. Take my yoke upon you and learn from me, for I am gentle and humble in heart, and you will find rest for your souls. For my yoke is easy and my burden is light." Matthew 11:28-30

HEAVEN

H — "He is close to the brokenhearted and saves those who are crushed in spirit." Psalm 34:18

E — "Everywhere Your Hand shall lead me, and Your right hand shall hold me." Psalm 139:10

A — "And God shall wipe away all tears from their eyes; and there shall be no more death, neither sorrow, nor crying, neither shall there be any more pain: for the former things are passed away." Revelation 21:4

V — "Verily, verily, I say unto you, He that heareth my word, and believeth on him that sent me, hath everlasting life, and shall not come into condemnation; but is passed from death unto life." John 5:24

E — "Even as the Son of man came not to be ministered unto, but to minister, and to give His life (as) a ransom for many." Matthew 20:28

N — "No one comes to the Father except through me." Jesus states: "I am the way, the truth, and the light." John 14:6

More about what God says Heaven will be like:

❤ Revelation 21:21-25

21 And the twelve gates were twelve pearls; every gate was of one pearl: and the street of the city was pure gold, as it were transparent glass.

22 And I saw no temple therein: for the Lord God Almighty and the Lamb are the temple of it.

23 And the city had no need of the sun, neither of the moon, to shine in it: for the glory of God did lighten it, and the Lamb is the light thereof.

24 And the nations of them which are saved shall walk in the light of it: and the kings of the earth do bring their glory and honor into it.

25 And the gates of it shall not be shut at all by day: for there shall be no night there.

❤ Matthew Chapter 6: 19-21

19 Lay not up for yourselves treasures upon earth, where moth and rust does corrupt, and where thieves break through and steal:

20 But (instead) lay up for yourselves treasures in heaven, where neither moth nor rust doth corrupt, and where thieves do not break through nor steal:

21 For where your treasure is, there will your heart be also.

HEAVEN WILL BE BEYOND OUR WILDEST DREAMS AND EXPECTATIONS!

💕 Revelation 22:1-5 - Additional about Heaven

Revelation Chapter 22:

1 And he showed me a pure river of water of life, clear as crystal, proceeding out of the throne of God and of the Lamb.

2 In the midst of the street of it, and on either side of the river, was there the tree of life, which bare twelve manner (kinds) of fruits, and yielded her fruit every month: and the leaves of the tree were for the healing of the nations.

3 And there shall be no more curse: but the throne of God and of the Lamb shall be in it; and his servants shall serve him:

4 And they shall see his face; and his name shall be in their foreheads.

5 And there shall be no night there; and they need no candle, neither light of the sun; for the Lord God giveth them light: and they shall reign for ever and ever.

💕 "I am the resurrection and the life. Those who believe in Me, even though they die, will live, and everyone who lives and believes in Me will never die.   John 11:25-26

Here are the lyrics to the most beautiful song by Chris Tomlin, but you really need to listen to the song to give it justice—you will be so happy that you did!

He Shall Reign Forevermore

In the bleak mid-winter, all creation groans
For a world in darkness, frozen like a stone
Light is breaking,
In a stable for a throne

And He shall reign forevermore, forevermore
And He shall reign forevermore, forevermore
Unto us a child is born

And He shall reign forevermore, forevermore
If I were a wise man, I would travel far
And if I were a shepherd, I would do my part
But poor as I am I will give to Him my heart

Here within a manger lies
The One who made the starry skies
This baby born for sacrifice
Christ, the Messiah

Into our hopes, into our fears
The Savior of the world appears
The promise of eternal years
Christ, the Messiah

And He shall reign forevermore, forevermore
Unto us a child is born
The King of kings and Lord of lords
And He shall reign forevermore, forevermore.

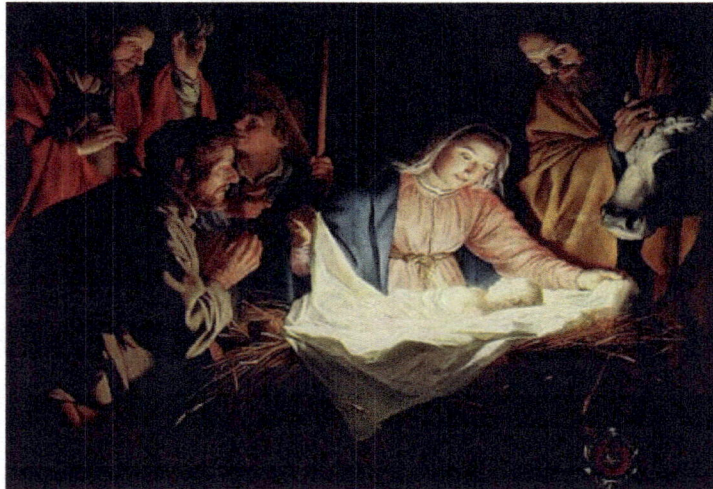

BIBLE VERSES OF ENCOURAGEMENT FOR YOU

"Be strong and courageous. Do not fear or be in dread of them, for it is the LORD your God who goes with you. He will not leave you or forsake you." Then Moses summoned Joshua and said to him in the sight of all Israel, "Be strong and courageous, for you shall go with this people into the land that the LORD has sworn to their fathers to give them, and you shall put them in possession of it. " - Deuteronomy 31:6-7

"Fear thou not for I am with you; be not dismayed for I am your God. I will help you, I will strengthen you, I will uphold you with My mighty right hand." Isaiah 41:10

"The LORD himself goes before you and will be with you; he will never leave you nor forsake you. Do not be afraid; do not be discouraged." Deuteronomy 31:8

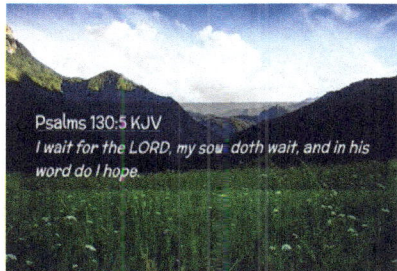

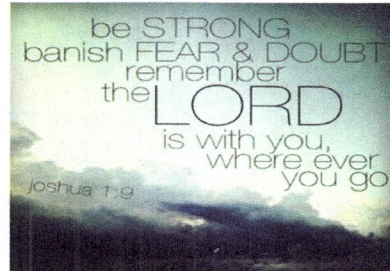

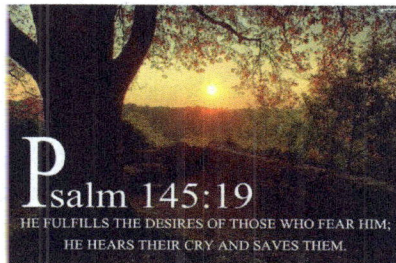

HEAVEN IS FOR EVERYONE

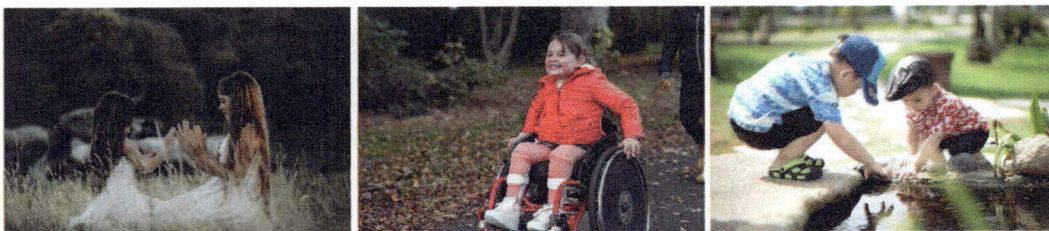

We can sleep on the beach,

or dive to the bottom of the ocean with no fear

HE CREATES EVERYTHING WITH LOVE

HIS STUNNING CREATIONS WILL LEAVE YOU SPEECHLESS!

Artwork by Iv'an Tam'as – Courtesy of Internet

"Eye has not seen, nor ear heard, nor have entered into the heart of man the things which God has prepared for those who love Him." I Corinthians 2:9

WE ARE THE FLOWERS IN HIS GARDEN

Praying for many blessings for you and your loved ones.

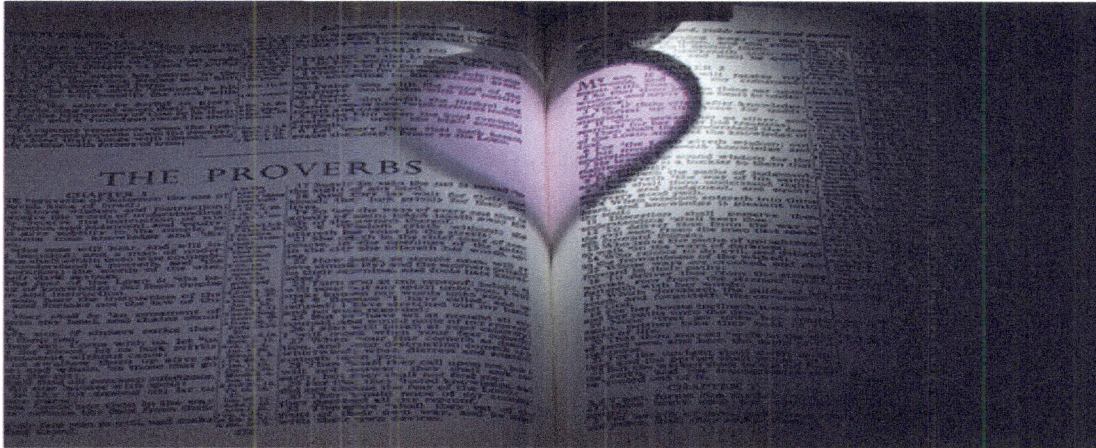

PERSONALIZED JUST FOR YOU:

❤ "FOR GOD SO LOVED_____ THAT HE GAVE HIS

(Your name)

ONLY BELOVED SON, SO THAT_____ BELIEVES IN

(Your name)

HIM WILL NOT PERISH BUT WILL HAVE EVERLASTING LIFE!"   John 3:16

   *It really is that simple: He invites, you accept. Follow Him and give everything to Him—all the heartaches, confusion, indecisions, frustration, panic, struggles, all the negatives. The second Satan slams you with anything at all, just give it to God right that moment—don't hang on to it because He can handle it!

Eternal life will be yours with many blessings every day, also each time you talk with Him, pray with Him, study with Him, have devotions with Him. Because God says it, He is truth, and we believe it.

God's Dove of peace – we are all in His hands.

SPECIAL INFORMATION FOR YOU:

*Additional books by Author Trenee' Zweigle, RN - available on Amazon:

-Teen Prayer Book = Love and encouragement for Teens

-Never Give Up –Encouragement for Women

-God Answers Your Prayers

-Cry Out to Jesus – Still Standing (With God)

-Women's Bible Promises for you from God's Heart – Prayer booklet

-Spiritual Warfare for Women

-Kitty Miracles at 7th Street Clubhouse (Humorous Kitty stories)

Free Bible study guides for you (taken *directly* from the bible) and much more:

https://www.amazingfacts.org/bible-study/free-online-bible-school

Website: https://www.amazingfacts.org   (Hundreds of free videos available for you here and on Youtube.)

Additional amazing information:
https://www.youtube.com/user/AmazingFacts

*Amazing Facts Series by Doug Batchelor.

Note: This educational series began with a hippy living in a cave for years who didn't believe in anything. Many years later he was given a bible, but accidentally dropped it in the river. He fished it out and even though wrinkled he kept reading page after page. Through reading it he discovered and fell in love with God, Jesus, and the Holy Spirit.

Doug Batchelor dedicated his life to God and eventually became a world known pastor, ministering around the world providing seminars, study groups, educational series, bible studies and sermons. He goes specifically only by the Bible, not his own speculation or anyone else's— just as it should be.

We are praying for you!

None of us want to miss out on the beauty of Heaven, the Majesty and love of God, or the best hug and life we will ever receive!

Many Blessings in your journey and new life (no matter how long you've been a Christian, or if you're just beginning) with God, your Father. You are His child forever; you are already in His heart.

YOUR NOTES:

Made in the USA
Columbia, SC
26 April 2023